COTTONMOUTHS

BY: ERIC ETHAN

Gareth Stevens Publishing
MILWAUKEE

For a free color catalog describing Gareth Stevens' list of high-quality books, call 1-800-542-2595 (USA) or 1-800-461-9120 (Canada). Gareth Stevens' Fax: 1-414-225-0377.

Library of Congress Cataloging-in-Publication Data

Ethan, Eric.
    Cottonmouths / by Eric Ethan.
      p. cm. — (Fangs! an imagination library series)
    Includes index.
    Summary: Describes what cottonmouths, or water moccasins, look like, what they eat, where they can be found, how they defend themselves, the danger from their bites, and the outlook for their future.
    ISBN 0-8368-1430-4
    1. Agkistrodon piscivorus—Juvenile literature. [1. Water moccasin. 2. Poisonous snakes. 3. Snakes.] I. Title.
II. Series: Ethan, Eric. Fangs! an imagination library series.
QL666.069E85   1995
597.96—dc20   95-19262

Published in 1995 by:
Gareth Stevens Publishing
1555 N RiverCenter Drive, Suite 201
Milwaukee WI 53212 USA

Original Text: Eric Ethan
Series Design: Shari Tikus
Cover Design: Karen Knutson
Photo Credits: All photos © Joe McDonald except Page 21 © Gail Shumway

Printed in the United States of America
1 2 3 4 5 6 7 8 9 99 98 97 96 95

TABLE OF CONTENTS

WHAT ARE COTTONMOUTHS?

Cottonmouths are poisonous snakes found in the southeast part of the United States. Their scientific name is *Agkistrodon piscivorus* (ag KISS tro dan pis ki VOR us). This means hooked-tooth fish-eater. Cottonmouths have curved fangs and eat fish. Their common name comes from the white cotton-like color on the inside of their mouths. Cottonmouths are also called water moccasins.

The Cottonmouth gets its name from the pinkish white on the inside of its mouth.

WHAT DO THEY LOOK LIKE?

Cottonmouths have flat wide heads shaped like a triangle. They have heavy bodies and grow to a length of 30-45 inches (76-114 cm). The inside of the cottonmouth's mouth is a bright pinkish white.

Most cottonmouths are olive or brown colored with black cross bands. Their bodies are covered by flat, tough plates called scales. Each scale has a ridge running down the middle of it. Snakes must shed their skin as they grow larger. When snakes shed their old skin becomes dry and thin. Then a new skin forms and they crawl out of their old one.

A cottonmouth found in a Florida swamp.

WHERE ARE THEY FOUND?

Cottonmouths can be found from southern Virginia to Missouri and in all southeastern United States. They live in ponds, swamps, and near rivers. Most often they burrow holes in the muddy ground near the water. Sometimes they move into dens made by other animals like muskrats.

When it grows colder, cottonmouths will move to higher ground away from water. They make new dens there to **hibernate** in until it is warm again.

Cottonmouths spend a lot of time in water.

SENSES AND HUNTING

Cottonmouths are **predators**. This means they must eat other animals to stay alive. But cottonmouths cannot hear well. They cannot see very well either.

A cottonmouth uses its tongue to find prey. Each time the tongue flicks out of the mouth, it takes a sample of the air and ground around it. In the cottonmouth's mouth the **Jacobson's organ analyzes** what the tongue picks up. This tells the cottonmouth what is near.

The tongue on this young cottonmouth is just sticking out of its mouth.

Cottonmouths have small pits between their eyes and nose. These are called **loreal pits**. They allow the snake to detect warm-blooded prey even at night.

Cottonmouths hunt during the day or night. On land they often ambush prey. This means they wait quietly in one place until an animal comes near before they strike. Cottonmouths can swim quickly. In water they will go after fish and frogs. Cottonmouths can bite under water.

Can you see the loreal pit between this cottonmouths eye and nose?

WHAT DO THEY EAT?

Because cottonmouths hunt on both land and water, they eat many different things. On land they eat small **mammals** like rats and mice. In water they eat frogs and fish of all types.

No matter what they catch, cottonmouths swallow it head first. This makes it easier to swallow. Snakes can open their mouths very wide. This allows cottonmouths to kill and swallow fish bigger around than they are.

This cottonmouth is eating a fish it has caught.

SELF-DEFENSE

Fully grown cottonmouths have few enemies except humans and alligators. On land, cottonmouths will move away from danger. They do not want to waste **venom** on animals they cannot eat.

Most cottonmouths are well **camouflaged**. If they lay still, it can be difficult to see them. People can accidentally step on them in areas near swamps and rivers.

An alligator attacking a large cottonmouth in the Florida Everglades.

COTTONMOUTH BITES

Cottonmouths open their mouths very wide as a warning. When cottonmouths bite, they inject venom through their fangs. Fangs are very sharp hollow teeth. In a fully grown cottonmouth the fangs are about 1/2 inch (1.3 cm) long. When not in use, a cottonmouth's fangs are folded back to the top of its mouth.

Cottonmouths can inject a lot of venom with each bite. Rattlesnake bites are more common in North America, but cottonmouth bites can be deadly. The bite of an adult cottonmouth can easily kill a person.

Can you see this cottonmouth's fangs

UNUSUAL FACTS

Cottonmouths are more tolerant of cold weather than other snakes. They are one of the last snakes to hibernate and one of the first to come out in the spring.

Poisonous snakes usually have only two fangs at one time. But cottonmouths have been captured that have four working fangs.

Most cottonmouths live ten to fifteen years, but in zoos where they are well cared for, they can live twenty years or more.

On land, cottonmouths bite and release their prey. But in water, cottonmouths bite and hold on to keep the fish from swimming too far away for the snake to find again.

A cottonmouth coiled on a mass of floating leaves in a Florida swamp.

THE FUTURE

Most people never see cottonmouths. These snakes live in swamps and wet areas away from most people. Alligators will kill cottonmouths if they catch them, but they do not catch many.

The biggest danger to cottonmouths today is loss of **habitat**. Swamps and wet areas are sometimes drained for farms or places for people to live. This causes the food cottonmouths eat to go away and they lose their place to live.

Today there are fewer cottonmouths in states like Texas, Oklahoma, and Missouri than there once were.

GLOSSARY

analyze (AN a lize) - To separate something into its parts to study them.

camouflage (KAM 0 flazh) - Colors or patterns that helps an animal look like the ground around it.

habitat (HAB i tat) - The place where an animal is normally found.

hibernate (HI ber nate) - To spend the winter in a deep sleep.

Jacobson's organ (JAY kob sons OR gan) - A special pouch in a snakes mouth that analyzes what the tongue picks up.

loreal pit (LOR e all) - A small hole near a snake's nose that can see infrared light.

mammal (MAM el) - A warm-blooded animal that has a backbone.

predator (PRED a tor) - An animal that lives by killing and eating other animals.

venom (VE nom) - The poison of snakes.

INDEX

PLACES TO WRITE FOR MORE INFORMATION

American Society of Ichthyologists and Herpetologists
US National Museum
Washington, DC 20560

Copeia
American Society of Herpetologists
34th Street and Girard Avenue
Philadelphia, PA 19104

Herpetologists' League
1041 New Hampshire Street
Lawrence, KS 66044

Herpetological
1041 New Hampshire Street
Lawrence, KS 66044